21 QUESTIONS

YOU MUST ANSWER TO

SUCCEED IN CORPORATE AMERICA

A GUIDE TO SUCCESS

Demishia Wright

Pocket Ace
Publishing

Thank you for
always empowering
me
MOM

Detavius so you will
know how to start
your journey

#1. What Is Your Confidence Level?
#2. Are You A Subject Matter Expert?
#3. Do you Network Up?
#4. Is your resume updated and efficient?
#5. Are you the Homecoming Queen at work?
#6. Do you know who is in the Building?
#7. What is Your Career Path?
#8. Do you know why you should never have a Supervisor?
#9. Do you eat Like a Boss?
#10. Do you know Sports?
#11. Do you read and comprehend all Emails?
#12. Where does your work feed come from?
#13. Are you a Corporate Hustler?
#14. What is your company's culture?
#15. Who are the managers/employees on the move?
#16. Do you have a mentor?
#17. Do you ask questions?
#18. Do you have and use LinkedIn?
#19. Are you in proper business associations?
#20. Are you Learning and Growing?
#21. Do you have a strategy?

Foreword

Work hard! This is a very common piece of advice given in terms of what it takes to succeed. However, hard work is only one piece of the success maze. The written career milestones are for the most part straightforward. You are here and these are the milestones to get you to the next level. What is not as obvious are those things that are not codified or documented. As an officer in the United States Army, I know the key developmental schools and assignments at rank in order to be competitive within my cohort group. I know because regulation tells me so. The things I had to learn on my own and with the assistance with mentors and leaders who care.

Speaking and writing are two important skills for senior leaders, yet it these were skills not emphasized early in my career as an officer. It was not until I became a commander of a unit, did I realize the importance of public speaking and writing in gaining and earning credibility. Another example is self-promotion. As a commander, I was once told that I needed to market myself more. In my mind if I can handle issues at my level without getting my superiors involved, then I have done my job. Not quite. This particular superior appreciated that I strove to solve issues at my level. What he meant was he wanted awareness of the issues I took care of, to appreciate my problem solving capacity and creativity.

21 Questions, is not meant to be an exhaustive or comprehensive list of questions. Rather is a good framework for self-awareness. Simply it is short inventory of one's current position in the corporate world (but is applicable for the workplace in general). When reviewing these questions the reader should take stock of where they are in the success maze, determine where they need to be and, begin mapping a path that will take them to the end. Demishia complied these questions based on her experience in the corporate world. I am not in the corporate world, and these questions made me review my own map.

Iana J. Daniels
CPT, US Army
Instructor, United States Army Engineer School

What Is Your Confidence Level?

Confidence is defined as a feeling of self-assurance arising from one's appreciation of one's own abilities or qualities. In the workplace you cannot come off as someone who second guesses yourself. You need to learn to make logical decisions confidently and stand by them. That does not mean you are always right. What it does demonstrate is that you are confident in your knowledge and decision making skills which can take you far in any environment. People follow those who know where they are going, even if it's not the right place to be. They just do.

With confidence, you have won before you have started.
Marcus Garvey

Are You A Subject Matter Expert?

Subject Matter Experts are those who have knowledge about a process, system, or product that is uncommon and often times not documented. To excel you need to become great at something. Your direct management, peers, and customers should be able pin point you as the go to person for something. Being a subject matter expert does not imply that you don't know or understand other aspects of your business unit or organization, it just says you have vested enough time to learn something to be a value when needed. Once you have mastered one process, system, or product you naturally expand to become a subject matter expert in another eventually mastering it from end to end.

Do you Network Up?

Networking is an essential part of life, and always has been. You need to network up! Networking up simply means you don't just go meet random people and think your goals will get accomplished. You need to be more strategic with your networking. You have to put yourself in the right place at the right time. Are you networking with people in your industry, with managers at work, people with experience in your field or profession, those who have been there before you etc? Some great places to start should be alumni, organizational and industry events.

When I compliment you, I compliment myself, because I am who I associate with."
— Jarod Kintz

Is your resume updated and efficient?

Is your resume tailored to positions you are seeking out. Your resume should not be a one size fits all situations. You should have several versions of your resume that shift and transform. Resumes should be strategic and intentional. There are many resources and examples available for how to structure your resume. There is a simple way to tell if your resume works. If you are getting callbacks and interviews, it is working If not you need to regroup your resume and career search methods.

Are you the Homecoming Queen at work?

Being popular for social reasons only is not good. You do not need to be everyone's buddy and be at every social event you are invited to by co-workers. You can be polite and kind without being most popular. You want to be known for your work ethic, skills, and knowledge not for how people feel about you. You want to build your personal brand as a subject matter expert not the one who plans the best company potluck.

Do you know who is in the Building?

If your office is located in some obscure location far away from the decision makers, Houston we have a problem. Understand how important your position/job/location is to your company. If you are in a building with decision makers know who they are, be able to identify them, and understand the best conversation to have with them if you happen to be in an elevator or sitting near them.

"To acquire knowledge, one must study; but to acquire wisdom, one must observe."
— Marilyn Vos Savant

What is Your Career Path?

Are you in a position that actually has a path to greatness? Is there a plan to get you from point A to B to C to D in your company or organization? Make sure you are not just working a "dead end" job and you are in place where there is actually opportunity to thrive. Every job is not a career. Understand whether you are in a career position or just a job that has no forward movement. This sometimes can be tricky because jobs can pay really well and be great, but have no upward mobility.

Do you know why you should never have a Supervisor?

Supervisors are not there to make sure you are learning, growing, and progressing in your profession. A supervisor is normally found in a massive activity done by many. A Supervisor is the person who supervises a person that is doing a specific activity. They are more like overseers to make sure a menial job is being completed by a certain time each day. You want to move to a place where someone is responsible for managing your skills and talents that match company objectives and goals.

Do you eat Like a Boss?

People observe and judge you just on what and how you order your food. If you are a picky eater that is fine, but do not put that on display when at company functions. Do not be the whiner, the complainer, or the one who appears uncultured because you are tooting your nose up to the food. It comes off as ignorant and does not help you make a good impression.

Do you know Sports?

Religion, Politics, and Reality TV should not be topics you discuss at work especially with upper management. If you want to spark casual light hearted conversation to show your personality or to fill dead space, sports is normally a safe place. My boss always has on my college's rival team shirt and loves to stop and chit chat with me about it. I make sure that I throw in what project I am working etc. while having those chit chats. Find a safe topic that is not controversial to talk about at work.

Do you read and comprehend all Emails?

Emails can drive us all crazy but they are a great source of information. We all get emails from those group distribution emails that are not addressed to us. Do you just ignore them? Well stop it and start reading them. It is important to understand everything that flows to you. Take a moment to understand what that email is why you should or should not be getting it. Remember your objective is to become a subject matter expert and following the email thread can lead you to great information and to who the key players and decision makers are.

When you pay attention to boredom it
gets unbelievably interesting.
Jon Kabat-Zinn

Where does your work feed come from?

Where does what you do fit into the big picture of your company's products or services. Are you a core component or someone that can be outsourced? Where does your work feed come from and then where does it go next. Understanding the end to end processes are critical to understanding what you should learn next and what teams you should shadow and understand.

Are you a Corporate Hustler?

I am a Corporate Hustler because there must be activity and movement in my career because they do not last forever. You must find your worth and ask for your value and more. The word hustle when used as a verb means to force (someone) to move hurriedly or unceremoniously in a specified direction. You must force your corporation to move your career and paychecks in the direction you want. I know it sounds harsh but corporate America is not for everyone. Are you the first to volunteer for special projects, to cross train, to make sure company objectives are met? Are you keeping up with your industry, are you a leader, do you get results? If so you are a Corporate Hustler and you need to get your worth.

What is your company's culture?

Understanding the company's culture and political environment of your organization is important. You cannot just speak freely to any one just because you think they like you. A company's culture is a combination of many things including its vision, values, norms, systems, symbols, language, assumptions, beliefs, and habits. Understanding if your office is formal or informal and how to navigate its landscape is important.

We will never—and I mean never —turn our backs on our employees.
-Howard Schultz, Starbucks:

Who are the managers/employees on the move?

You don't want to work for a dead beat manager or one that is not interested in being in the thick of things. When your team or manager is always off the grid and not involved in current issues and projects this can make your career path more difficult. You want a manager or to belong to team that is taking on projects and making impacts in the organization. If your manager is a go getter they will make sure their direct reports are getting exposure and opportunities. Also model yourself after co-workers that are on the move in the company.

Do you have a mentor?

Mentors are a valuable human resource for your career and life. They do not have to work in your department or even company to be effective in your career. Finding a mentor can take time and is a give/take relationship but it is something you need to begin working on or cultivating. It would be good to get one that is in your industry and that has been where you want to go.

"Tell me and I forget, teach me and I may remember, involve me and I learn."
— Benjamin Franklin

Do you ask questions?

Do you sit around pretending that you know what is going on? Do you sit in meetings not understanding what is going on, yet ask no questions? I guarantee you are not the only one therefore STOP IT. Do not be afraid to ask relevant questions to topics being discussed. If you are not sure what to ask, then simply ask for a piece of information to be stated again. This technique may prompt a question. Ask for the background information or if they mention a process or system, you are not aware of, SAY SOMETHING.

The art and science of asking questions is the source of all knowledge.
Thomas Berger

Do you have and use LinkedIn?

Your social media presence is important. How you are presenting yourself on platforms like LinkedIn can make the difference, if you are getting the opportunities and information you need. It is the first impression recruiters and human resource managers have of you sometimes. Often people will not even contact you personally but will make a decision to recommend you for jobs and opportunities they know of because of this profile.

Are you in proper business associations?

This is a specific type of networking that helps you automatically target the people you need to know. Understanding who the movers and shakers are, and events to be at, can all be discovered when you attend business and industry association and organization meetings and events. This is a great source to find out what companies are hiring, what the industry trends are, and who to get to know. It is a great place to find a mentor and just meet likeminded people who run in the same industry as you.

Are you Learning and Growing?

Learning and growing should be the goal each day. Strive to be better than you were yesterday in life and in your profession. A job is just a job but your profession stays with you for a lifetime. Your profession can transition from place to place, job to job, opportunity to opportunity if you allow it to. Always keep up with the best practices and techniques in your field.

I am not afraid of storms for I am learning how to sail my ship.
Louisa May Alcott

Do you have a strategy?

Have you calculated the next move(s) you need
to make to get to the next level in your
profession or industry? Always have a plan
that not only increases your knowledge and
expertise but is a map or guide to success. Be
ready to move positions and take on new tasks.
Understand what education level is needed to
progress your Corporate Hustle! Think outside
the box! This can be certifications,
conferences, or formal degrees or a
combination of experiences that can get you to
next level.
You know what they say- Stay Ready

However beautiful the strategy, you
should occasionally look at the results.
Winston Churchill

About The Author

Demishia Wright is a Corporate Entrepreneur who has found her worth inside and out of Corporate America. Demishia has a passion for helping people get their money. She has learned you must shift your mindset to move beyond an average mediocre life. She is a graduate of Georgia State University with a degree in Marketing. Demishia is currently an IT Professional for a major Fortune 500 Company, Social Media Strategist, a leader, Income Coach, and a Mother! She owns several brands and is still climbing the Corporate ladder using these proven techniques and habits.

" I am proven leader who loves to help Young Professionals find their worth Inside and Outside of Corporate America"

www.demishia.com

Where to Find Us

Visit
www.demishia.com

Join Our Invitation Only Facebook Group where we
discuss career strategies, techniques, and more .
Corporate Hustlers

Discount Code: 21Questions
To Register for
our Corporate Hustle 101 Seminar
www.demishia.com

www.ingramcontent.com/pod-product-compliance
Lightning Source LLC
Chambersburg PA
CBHW070800180526
45168CB00004B/1688